PERIL

AS ARCHITECTURAL

ENRICHMENT

Hazel

White

Peril

AS ARCHITECTURAL

ENRICHMENT

KELSEY STREET PRESS

KELSEY STREET PRESS

2824 KELSEY STREET BERKELEY, CA 94705

INFO@KELSEYST.COM WWW.KELSEYST.COM

DISTRIBUTED BY SMALL PRESS DISTRIBUTION

[510] 524-1668 OR [800] 869-7553

LIBRARY OF CONGRESS CATALOGING-IN-PUBLICATION DATA

WHITE, HAZEL.

PERIL AS ARCHITECTURAL ENRICHMENT / HAZEL WHITE.

P. CM.

ISBN 978-0-932716-76-7 (ACID-FREE PAPER)

I. TITLE.

PS3623.H5756P47 2011

811'.6—DC22

2011010807

DESIGN AND COMPOSITION BY QUEMADURA

PRINTED ON ACID-FREE, RECYCLED PAPER

IN THE UNITED STATES OF AMERICA

FOR MATT AND JAKE

The presence of the world is precisely the presence of its flesh to my flesh.

MAURICE MERLEAU-PONTY

Truant

The canopy of a tree, say a poplar, like a round house, removes the site of vulnerability—the obvious entrance and back with no protection.

Privacy can creep about in the leaves and below them, hang here as lungs on the outside.

Isometrics will show the interior corridors, ways to habituate oneself to curvature.

To take a house up on stilts also, above that first tall leap that allows a beast into the tree and onto her.

Pocket any peril that's evaded; swan warm on the clear lake. Or look out at it, especially nice between ornamented columns, to set a mid-distance that invokes one's own grandeur.

Another pleasure from up, aerially, to see along the tops of hedges and ski, sunned, on top of it all, goodbye to all the damned crannies.

An armchair by a tall fireplace and look out entirely horizontally
   —through glass windows over lawn floors, receptacles of light's courtesy.

Peril can be pushed into the distance, into a consolidation, like a town, although it's bound to have one messenger running.

Truant on the tree's pinnacle, missing the last chance to go to school and socialize as normal.

To be beginning architecture over

A cradle of deciduous structure mocks a balancing pole of thinking. There's an appropriate height for pleasure, higher struts into peril.

Stunt-girl can't untether from the fulcrum of the farmhouse roof; see how fiercely Mother ties trussing strings. The growth on the tree could never be so one-sided.

Yet a vertical axis dominates, apically, receiving the light first, sashays it.

At Combray the steeple is a sign of art amid miles of trees, a point of habitation. Traveling aborigines placed a pole to mark an overnight stopping place, and when one day it broke they died.

Up, life states itself in the number of hedges, the parcels of pasture, the vegetable garden and each of four dozen newly planted brassica, plus the one swan happy on her placid horizontal.

Sky reveals ——, yet there's danger in perpetual soaring, to insist that the most deeply loved place is invisible.

The unrepresentational lies behind our staring out the window instead of "telling ourselves flat."

The sky is not a cup; so unpredictably generative, and it's hard to be cold and welcome surprises. Besides, how enjoyable is it to be linked to an accident-causing force?

Viewed between twigs, intimacy appears mathematical, reconciliatory, but don't talk of union, too many bifurcations.

A reciprocity of light and leaves rushing toward each other unthinkable while anger storms the kitchen. Four directions at once.

More comforting is a sky that touches down where you want it, in a blue flower, say. And I do love inertia and geometry, as in a symmetry of sun and rain, not too inevitably propelled forward.

>   —Sip mirrored blue, on the lake, with much less disordering.

The eye and then the heart give themselves over to a soft bowl. A way of opening wings without pain: reveal a broad, assertive breast (keep legs forward and away) and uncurl musculature by patching with feverfew daisies that branch and rebranch into plenty.

Self-sprung sets the story on the move again. Arms wide. For example, she, by chance, was seen kissing him.

Contemplating landing, the eye searches the distance to the gravel, wanting no new emotion. A fearless courtyard evenly lit or a pond grown over.

The frame from above demarcates a real situation. How to descend into it? Stencil the way down, branch beneath branch, each one sturdier.

Peril in going down diagonally, an arrow, short, on the dirt, no camouflage
      or flat onto the lawn near a window to the indoors—so close.

Rather,
          drift with conviction as a bee into marigolds, be captured, click into
          [miniature].

Scale up and scuff this.
Shimmy, knot by
knot

into corolla,
pelvis, den/dell,
beneath the skirts.

Grow tall and tipping
into blue chicory-like flowers
so plural at the edge of fields.

Responding, a tomboy by design, one pours oneself, etiolates—
until frightened suddenly of what is certain not to happen later. Truancy becomes too
prospect dominant.

Stop a moment.
Recall a comfort such as recessed eaves or a bushy eyebrow. Then try to exaggerate
and free-fall.

Diseased with an ache, for a briefer narrative, one's ragged gold marigolds are a native country without borders.

BBC reports a pollen grain may travel to nineteen thousand feet and three thousand
miles. That's so nutritious! Turn on the dance floor and the dress will fly out in a circle. Into old velvet twilights and you'll see.

A *plan libre* is its openings, though the cone of vision is achieved through abandonment. Le Corbusier's structures, for example, reveal unusually generous, I'd say harrowing, transparency. Just how safe is it to leave a female figure in an open space?

The distinction between her plight and the farm architecture is crisp. It lodges in her throat. She surrenders the back of herself.

A long vista weakening the space behind the eye.

Panorama, equal to exile. Absurd therefore to nest here.

Unbuilt Garden

Break the conviviality when visitors get off the bus; that's what Richard Haag, land-scape architect, wanted. Four linked gardens: this one, the garden of planes, crisp in form (unbuilt). Haag pauses, mouth open . . . "You have to come around the big mound and then . . .
Slap!"

In a landscape too dangerous to be comprehended on foot, mind builds curvature in the air. Smithson's dialectics of the sublime, parts of this poem, suspend it.

Up is a universal. "Give two-year-olds a bunch of milk crates, and they'll put them to-gether and climb. Every organism . . . as it develops an awareness beyond itself, its first move is to ascend" —Haag.

No matter where you stand, at least one surface of the unbuilt garden of planes is hidden. Seeing, anyway, engenders a false sense that all things are knowable.

Pollen Carrier

Half-inch snowdrop blossoms in lanceolate green brace offer solitariness that relates to January ice, sudden whiteness by brown water. A lively woman is led forward this way, from darker to lighter zones.

Luminous circumscription exists beneath the drops—call it a faintly blessed tableau, territory doused in milky generosity.

Proceeding through repetition of values, infinitely small differences create elasticity and eventually a clearing.

An architecture of widespread pleasure? In the green, within arboreal customs. All the way home, Sister falls in the ditch.

Low in the airspace, on a pillow crown, gazes into a nave of green stems and tracery. There's joy in the conjunction of high and low spaces.

(Not yet supine near turquoise water. It would be careless at this point to name everything in that joining place between blue and green with one term.)

In times of peace, approaching a lily, after an initial greeting in the narrowing hall-way, one might descend toward saturation, into petal parlors where light and dark curl over one on the inside.

Somewhere in the drop is a flare that suggests an interior staircase and an invitation to be a pollen carrier.

     —Even the bulge in the calyx speaks to an ability to hang out over this. To bear out shape, one must get up and into it.

At Heathrow—rocked by how her nonchalance can blur a space's basic order. Peril downgraded to disappointment, an undramatic site.

Permission to cry, since it is impervious—a flower's continuous infantile feeding on daylight, membranes suckling on synthesis to heal by architectural means.

A flower

swallows a quarrel—

drop between petals like a seamstress into fabric, through

organic pleats of unending enclosure.

Go down and on. Allow invisibility.

Fall.

The deepest terrace, skylighted beneath pistils, might be an opaque rose
basket, as in the case of anemones and tulips. Grandmother was seen swinging
through knee-high blue forget-me-nots in the orchard, the sun dazed on the blue
cornflowers on her dress spreading over everything held and
spilled. Later I'll want to go for a
run.

A wild briar in a hedgerow opens its scenting miniature dishes delicately among the
cuts—cuts, sorry. The hedger splits a tree trunk so it cracks and topples, thereby making
the boundary of his agriculture lawful; reliably, shoots grow from the cuts, but he doesn't
see that the growth is intentional. Whereas "may-grow"
is a trick: only innocents, such as housewives and fairies, believe
a bundle of twigs plugged into the hedge may
grow.

A flower swallows by means of a spasm

female

jelly bone

tissue

unthinking the muscular.

Roll inside into the pollen chamber, view the
pink-cream curdle of gender. Here the time is always ripe for
curliness.
Breathe in, so privately, the pink.
Traces of blood, fragrance rinsed with rain, and nectaries
hidden deeply, away from evaporation.

Acquiring pollen is sedulous. The lilting flower
may substitute human movement, murmur like a photo
of a white-domed dovecot on a Victorian estate.
You can mop up the light daily.

Leaving the living room makes absolute sense when
there is no provision for plant material in the
architecture.

Fix a windbreak, venture into the garden walking: along the affirmative, beside black-green arboreal thickness, and through.

Up and into the sky light, such radial distances rolling,
foregrounded by cellular creaking.

Spill into and partner
lap to lap on the underside
with primrose petal or water.

Company switches
kingdoms:

plays with:
aphasia:

: Light to assist us in relation to our sentence.

Not romantic. Cow parsley, for example, uses very old rays, draws in what is now blind.

Can curl on oneself, counterclockwise north of the equator, one choice in this green, bright democracy. Vining—remember the medieval dread of nature, it keeps on coming toward one.

Run through it.

A rhizome underground, out of sight, an unbridled shape, an adventitious bud out to the side and preferring the horizontal. You see that tactic in bearded iris besides. Along and beneath is the first waywardness, a step in the dark uncovering a history of blood and chlorophyll.

When a potato arrives on the harvesting machine too ripe, it smells of animals from last night, sticky and glazed, makes one terrified of sudden frost.

The unzipped fly under the bridge in the dampest field; overplump touching its own prickles. Horned, bulbous.

If you must, plow memory under and pretend it was a stolen crop.

—In fear, pursuing botanical prudence, taking the feeling of home down into a taproot, a collection of enlivening prepositions your starch store.

Counter-circulating belts carry a potato up from the ground, because a potato rolls whereas dirt clods are more angular and fall through. Miraculous syntax of transport that reveals the sky and ends in a bag.

Dramatic complexity—kill for that. Instead widespread unending gritty repetition, here day in and out, so may never perch. No pleasure of differentiation. Not a site for exemplification either, which surely presupposes shelter and a view.

Does looking loosen in like-coloration? Go when horizontals are devoid of ornamentation to see whether there is anything complementary to bind or amuse. Just go ahead and suggest that the sky inclines slightly inward and there is nothing more closely spaced——.

When open to all sides like that: worm for what you are, what you illustrate so well, what can be eaten. Be compelled, to your advantage, to discern.

Even a falling body contributes appeal, because it retains evidence of its original configuration and what has been subtracted necessitates an act of mental completion of form. Sister, for example, in the schoolyard, turns the rope and jumps. We find interest in that exercise, similar to peering through foliage for what we can identify as a nest—or a tiger.

A loss, an absence of shape, a change of weather. Begin over. Re-state a low horizon and a high empty sky. Repeat it by and by and make a wish to write something beautiful.

Luckily, reflection does help scissor meaning, the way the floor of the Taj Mahal
subdivides recursively
to accommodate multiples of emptiness during a life,
separates the sublime from the beautiful,
circular domes over square rooms

and then in a sidestep breaks the planes and hurls the minarets
    into
      the rectangular garden pool—sky and all.

        Up goes a splash! Volume rigid with oxygen.

Fronting all that doubled longing is coming upon a clump of trees on a ridge, their diagonal boughs are Mother's skirts near us, and thus a landscape forms a fresh nest.

Greet it or fall down.

Anyhow, you'll see the surface dematerialize and change with the colors of the sky until the architecture on shore is no larger than a toy.

Brio brought back, inverted and immaterial, to the garden from which it had been removed.

Reflection Garden

Enclosing an existing pool with a tall hedge of yew, Haag coaxed blue into a valence
architecture can contain.

Sky

in a rectangular void
within a towering forest.

In less than a quarter acre,
with the trees
held
back
one space opens thoroughly to another.

Breath spreads far beyond the occasion.

Blue-green
glitters,   sweeps toward,

                            exchanges.

Prospect

Is it certain that the young protagonist will be home in time for tea? Re-situate to the bottom of a landscape where a slick road may yet form a phrase that has relation to leaping the fence. The only motion so far being in rain clouds.

The view is green and pleasant country under too much sky. Really. One desires a cheerful adventure tale and praise.

Not far from Hubbelrath or the Cherwell River, we can follow the pilgrimage route. The site extends for miles, with a T-intersection where I want to wait at dawn in a thin floral dress

posed as hitchhiker on a line like a string.

Upright, a signpost, blank because its back is to us, rises from dark soil across the road and tops out in the sky. It suggests evidence of a narrative threading through the smudged field alongside it where the crop has already ended.

Design pulls the eye and the imagination into motion, whatever you are thinking. At Rousham, a lichen-encrusted lion attacks a horse marking the axis, and the paths romp beside meadows of English daisies.

Ride along for free.

Overlays take care of ground falling away, smooth it into a dell and press upon you a mass of evergreens. Number 9 is the Cold Bath, Number 11, Temple of Echo. Where's the House?

Can a ruffle of white in the treetops on the horizon serve to capture anything at all—
my voice? We must not shelve this as a setting, a noun. Stories abound in quests so
I'll build you a sham, a ruin, place it on the skyline, call it Eye-Catcher.

Wait! A similarity links arms: twilight over distant fields, plus a carpet of primroses and gentians right here: it's doubly exposed that's speaking. Plenty in the act of dispersal.

After all, the concavity of the eye itself, its self-consciousness, is the little sister of the sky dome and of the throats of these flowers.

There's sphericity in up and down, freedom and shelter.

Roll hither and thither as you will.

Volumes squeeze the body, lighten it. Rhododendrons, for example, their large, oh-lordy blossoms so encrusted they hunt themselves and boss a boy and girl down.

All this landscape! And *Nymphaea* collaborate on the fish-stocked ponds: curl and rock, tipping out seed into the spaces among flowers, stars dotted and deep blue. Lick it.

That's the way passion tips like weather into—
The way a metal gate can open onto—

In summary, enfilading (a sequence of horizontal shots and equal, hedged enclosures) is not the answer. Cut away the middle ground of axial objects, the horticultural ones also. Stop yourself from advancing toward a cocky foursquare, artificially brimming with.

All that dominance and then the tedious harmony constructed of answering to that. Don't call it love! It's quickset: chiefly British; cuttings set in the ground to grow, especially in hedgerows.

Adventure may flicker in a break, say a cracked salt pan or a toadstool bitten into. A multihued bruise may elaborate a swindle.

Facts do not drop exactly into ———. It's necessary sometimes to tap oneself out of a treetop pretending to accompany the village clock striking the quarter hour.

What's so suspicious about sporting pods and glistening word spores?

What we are seeking allegedly lies on high ground. But the accident-prone shouldn't insist on the sheerest exploits, such as leaning over a high-rise balcony that opens on four sides
of the six sides of
space.

A topography falling
away
out of sight
is rarely entered.

Despite all the blue, there's no concentration of faith, either, on sands where tides recede under a disinterested sky and through a fractious sea.

Terrific speeds——are recorded
just at the point where equilibrium is up

set,

for example, Uluru (Ayers Rock) rising unexpectedly from a continent

or yourself laid out on the floor.

No flower wants to grow too tall.

Knocked
down
flat,   organisms   slow   their   pulse.

Shadows clarify on the flat, as if held. In her lap, a perfect leaf is plucked from hair.

A band of down, looping, like the carpenter whistling. Eddies floating dusty sub-
tleties in unlocked pieces.

No matter that it may be years before one can ripen and disperse oneself

                                                                    up.

                                                     back

Moss Garden

Arboreal disturbance, an excess of form—the hydrologic cycle present at every step and giant stumps abandoned—challenges the conception of ground as solid earth: terra firma sinks into terra incognita. Pull your breath in.

Haag's editing renders the disturbance more visible. Removed salmonberry reveals fallen trees. The scene vacillates between beauty and horror; it speaks.

Delicately textured ferns, moss, aralia, and huckleberry build scalar juxtaposition between ground and forest canopy—flutter: spore. Microscopic occurrences under hovering boughs. An aesthetic of inundation.

Haag turned from "doing anything more to the place."

Gravity, Ignobly

Throw the fruit out of the tree!

Lands, cra
ck,

    as one,

    including tongue

    to asphalt.

Messenger stopped.

Cheek flows cruelly over
mouth to one side,
eye heavily,
also
weight of
the ear.

From core
hangs
ignobly
from
waist
fallen

Dirt on the body.
Oops,
root follicles
drool
the animate
to blue,

maroon.

Tree
crashes
crushes floor   *Snap: snap: snap:*

Switch:
Life/death
beetles
(inside).

What plants do: in crisis, they change systems—take the greener future back just when—and then, intensely interior, thickening rather than reaching: they: seed.

Blanch to form a crevice; through corrugated topography, moisture may run, as through the tubular structures in a body, beginning at the mouth. Liquidity passes into the arch of the jaw, floats damaged cells.

Gathering-in-at-great-speed:

Habituation to vision was a form of repression in itself.
Tunneling, I recognize the incompatibility of truths within myself.

What can be gathered tenderly, in the way of weeds proliferating in a place suddenly well watered—clap for a Johnny-jump-up.

Dainty Bess, rosa amo, an open rose, hybrid, privately I lie in its lit concavities in clusters. Swing injured in the wind, lapsing. Rousham's Bunty House.

Lie down and rest, Sister says it. Spine rubbery, bones to fallen petals of lilacs, lych-nis, monkshood, laburnum, rue. I'll overgrow till the berry skins split. Satin twines from here; for while I talk and sleep, sweet Williams are budding at Moseley Old Hall in Staffordshire. I'm seeding in loose umbels and random agreements, but it's so hard to keep punctuating this—swan turns on the clear lake—because order causes trees to fall, officials anticipate disasters, insisting storms be part of their picture. I must trespass or violate, since it's in the budget and illness is constantly pruned out. Other-wise, what falls is prematurely repaired, opened to visitors, spits back a new alphabet.

Sunlight briefly over moss/redwood stops it.
Floor drenches roots, taunts the roof primitively.
Shut your eyes on the debris, its blooming, fat,
digestive ratio of down. Clotted toadstools choke
cold oxygen through, spawn the original falling.
Understory sloughs, sloughs bark, dust, piles bro-
kenness. Light wavers uselessly on a stem, while
limbs rot. Tunnels turn into what is not—unboning
caves of mutt green. Damn this cambium, dead
wood, bruising slump against a stump. Excrement
in spongy duff. Pain a scuffed mossed root; don't
stand on it! Here are beetles and no fruit. Bark and
gag. Rot worn clear through the story.

Extinct the ambulatory sequence, an overland of grass
passing—Has landscape ever saved us? Degrades
into a pompous waste of days, pilgrimage dropped
down into boxlike, black-emerald immobility. Fly-
ridden, regressive, vegetative habitat—pull the sky
right down here to mock it. Trounce these tight laws
—Why is forest, inside, not distance, the subject!
Trees so crowded, light so far above, water and dark
earth below.

What's lying at the surface between land and me, before mud-tongue muttered its prepositions?

How far to the bird marsh, its round, miniature islands of truancy?

What body, cut/dented/blue?

Spilled
and reproduces itself.

Hybridity's banal side: Seeding is commonplace. Grow tall like cow parsley, be umbelliferous host to seeds dangling, then fall and write the distances and architecture of dispersal

because beauty has forward momentum

Wind—
Birds—
Water—

Touching something smooth, Augustine began to think of God and music.

I would like to ride in the fur of animals.

Reflexively

expanding X
from left hip to right shoulder

left shoulder to right hip: the same

elasticity as leaf-light.

Vast before-me,

pliancy in guts.

No
Melancholy

BIRD MARSH

Hummocks of bird islands protected from human intrusion by a field of clear black water. Trumpeter swans fly over it, habitat understood through movement in space. Hop it. No melancholy. What a work of landscape architecture can do.

Land leeside of sylla
-bles that break at the shore.

Mid-distance: Indeterminacy so horizontal.

But circulation in the curvature of clouds—

tracked

/ dispersed

reciprocated

in the body.

BUILD

Pillow along, no asperities. Interval it: flower, treetop, grass, an ox-bow lake, a deeper ravine.

Spin encounters

as allées focus light.

ACKNOWLEDGMENTS

Some poems have appeared in *Denver Quarterly, Blink, Tarpaulin Sky* (online), and *Verse.* Sincere thanks to Bin Ramke, Amber DiPietra, Bhanu Kapil, Christian Peet, Brian Henry, and Andrew Zawacki for publishing them.

Thanks to Denise Newman, for insights, enthusiasm, and friendship.

Thanks to Jaime Robles and Susanne Dyckman for careful readings.

Special thanks to Kelsey Street co-founders Patricia Dienstfrey and Rena Rosenwasser and press members Ramsay Breslin, Amber DiPietra, Tiff Dressen, Amber Hopkins, and Val Witte for tremendous support.

And gratitude to Elyse Shafarman, Alexander Technique teacher, who for many years has explored how a body wants to move into space before habit and thought claim it.

The sequence of gardens by landscape architect Richard Haag mentioned on page 15 and later pages are at Bloedel Reserve on Bainbridge Island. Haag's work has inspired many people, and I owe a debt to Elizabeth Meyer, who has written so well about it. Lastly, my thanks to Grant Hildebrand for his book *Origins of Architectural Pleasure*, in which I found this book's title.

HAZEL WHITE

grew up on farms in the southwest of England. After finishing undergraduate degrees in philosophy and literature at Warwick University, she studied crop agriculture at Bridgwater College Center for Land Based Studies, and then, through University of California, Berkeley, Extension, landscape architecture. She's the author of eleven gardening books, published by Sunset Books and Chronicle Books, and for several years wrote a monthly column, "Living in the Landscape," 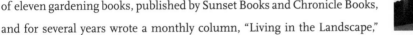 published by the *San Francisco Chronicle*. White graduated from the MFA Writing program at California College of the Arts in 2005. A chapbook of her poems, *Richter 14,* was published in 2010 by Deconstructed Artichoke Press. She lives in San Francisco with her partner and teenage son.